PATHWAY E

Following Jesus

LUKE 9-12

BY GORDON CHENG

matthiasmedia

Following Jesus
Pathway Bible Guides: Luke 9-12
© Matthias Media 2004

Matthias Media
(St Matthias Press Ltd. ACN 067 558 365)
PO Box 225
Kingsford NSW 2032 Australia
Telephone: (02) 9663 1478; Facsimile: (02) 9663 3265
International: +61-2-9663 1478; Facsimile +61-2-9663 3265
Email: info@matthiasmedia.com.au
Internet: www.matthiasmedia.com.au

ISBN 1 921068 24 8

Cover design and typesetting by Lankshear Design Pty Ltd.

CONTENTS

BEFORE YOU BEGIN

It may seem a strange place to launch a new Bible study—right in the middle of Luke's Gospel.

It's where the disciples finally work out that Jesus is no ordinary man. In Luke 9, Peter confesses that Jesus is "the Christ of God", the king that God has chosen to lead his people and rule his heavenly kingdom. It's exactly what anyone needs to realize before they can become a follower of Jesus. And in Luke's Gospel, the section that follows (from chapter 9 onwards) is all about what it means to be a follower of Jesus.

So this is a brilliant part of the Gospel to begin with if, like Peter, we have realized that Jesus must be our king, and we want to know what happens next.

What does it mean to be a follower of Jesus? Will we be powerful like him? Will we be rich? What's this about needing to 'take up our cross'? Once we decide Jesus is king, will we have to tell others?

And what about other parts of the Christian life? Christians are supposed to do good works, but what good works? Isn't Christianity just about trusting Jesus, and *not* about good works? What about prayer, money, and religious activity—where do they fit?

So then, this guide has two aims.

Firstly, the idea is to read this section of Luke's Gospel and be challenged to trust Jesus, and to see what that means for our lives and attitudes, including such important areas as prayer, wealth, and success.

Secondly, the plan is to provide a simple model of how to read the Bible for ourselves in a small group.

To help meet the second aim, each session begins with a brief discussion starter to help break the ice, and then dives straight into the Bible with questions about what the passage says. These opening questions usually have obvious and short answers straight out of the passage. After this, the questions deal more with what the passage means and how it applies.

The accompanying leader's notes (starting on page 39) give hints, tips and suggested answers, as well as background information and other passages to consult. However, the main idea is to stay with the passage in Luke that is set down—on the assumption that this particular part of God's word has something to say, and we ought to pay attention to what is in front of us.

The best way to use this guide is to read the set passage for yourself, and answer the questions briefly in your own time before you come to the group. When you then discuss your answers in the group, the work you've done by yourself will be a great help to yourself and to the other group members.

My prayer is that this guide to chapters 9 to 12 of Luke's Gospel will help us see Jesus more clearly and so trust him more firmly.

Gordon Cheng
May 2004

1. THE TURNING POINT

Luke 9:18-27

 **Getting started**

Pick one or more of the options below. Jesus being 'king' or 'lord' (that is, the boss) means:

○ He can do whatever miracle he wants.

○ He can say whatever he wants, and it will happen.

○ His closest followers will share his power.

○ Christians everywhere can share his power, if they have faith.

○ Christians can do Jesus' miracles, if they have faith.

Why did you pick your answer(s)?

🔆 Light from the Word

Read Luke 9:18-27.

1. In Luke 9:20, Peter says that Jesus is "the Christ of God" ("Christ" means king, lord or boss). In other words, Peter is saying that Jesus has enormous power and authority. If you were one of the disciples, what do you think Jesus might now predict:

    a. for himself?

    b. for anyone who follows him?

2. What does Jesus *actually* predict for himself (Luke 9:22)? (Note: 'the Son of Man' is Jesus' normal way of talking about himself.)

3. Can you think of any good reason why he doesn't want the disciples to tell people about him (Luke 9:21)?

4. What does Jesus promise for anyone who follows him (Luke 9:23-27)?

(How does this compare with your answer to question 1b above?)

5. Look again at Luke 9:23.

  a. What three things does someone have to do if they are going to follow Jesus?

    •

    •

    •

b. What do you think it means to 'take up your cross daily' (verses 24-26 will be helpful in answering this)?

c. What will happen if we:

- follow Jesus?

- don't follow Jesus?

6. If you have made the decision to follow Jesus, share in the group how the decision came about.

7. Think about the different areas of your life where you have to make the small daily decisions to 'deny yourself' and follow Jesus. Share in the group the areas that you find most difficult:

a. at home

b. at work

c. at church

d. in any other part of life

 ## To finish

Pick one point that you think is particularly important. How would you explain this point to a clever six-year-old?

 ## Pray

Pray for each other about the things you shared in question 7: those areas in which you struggle to follow Jesus each day.

2. HARVEST TIME

Luke 10:1-24

 Getting started

Pick one of the options below. Christianity will become popular and attract followers:

○ When Christians are not afraid to explain what they think.

○ When Christians start to live out what they believe, without ramming their ideas down other people's throats.

○ Both of the above.

○ On Judgement Day.

Explain why you picked your answer.

💡 Light from the Word

Read Luke 10:1-16.

1. What job does Jesus give to the 72 messengers?

2. The instructions Jesus gives mean that the 72 won't be slowed down by unnecessary baggage. What's the hurry (Luke 10:9, 11)?

3. What sort of response does Jesus tell the 72 to expect from people?

4. What will be the result for those who reject the kingdom of Jesus (Luke 10:12-15)?

5. In what ways do you think Christians today are like the 72 messengers, and in what ways are we not? Fill in the table below to help answer the question. If you think we are like the 72, indicate this with a tick. If we are not like the 72, indicate this with a cross. If you're not sure, put a question mark.

Command or example	Like the 72 = ✔ Unlike the 72= x*	Comment
e.g. 'followers of Jesus'	✔	e.g. 'Jesus is our Lord too, not just the Lord of the disciples.'
Sent out "two by two" to preach (10:1)		
Pray for labourers (10:2)		
Like "lambs in the midst of wolves" (10:3)		
"Carry no moneybag, no knapsack ..." (10:4)		
Give a greeting "Peace be to this house!" (10:5)		
Accept hospitality (10:7-8)		
Heal sick people (10:9)		
The message is: "The kingdom of God has come near to you" (10:9)		
"The one who hears you hears me" (10:16)		

* If you think that we are *both* like *and* unlike the disciples, put a tick *and* a cross. Give an explanation in your comment.

6. In Luke 10:17-20 the 72 report a great victory.

    a. What should we hope for when we tell others about Jesus?

    b. What should we be thankful for when we tell others about Jesus?

7. Now read Luke 10:21-24. From these verses, and from what we've seen earlier, what can we say about:

    a. God's role in people becoming Christians?

    b. our role in people becoming Christians?

 ## To finish

How would you use Luke 10 to encourage a nervous Christian friend to tell others about Jesus?

 ## Pray

Pray for friends who don't know Jesus. Share the names of these friends with other group members, and pray for them during the week.

3. LOVE YOUR NEIGHBOUR

Luke 10:25-37

 **Getting started**

In your day-to-day life, who would you consider a neighbour? Who would you not consider a neighbour? Why?

Light from the Word

Read Luke 10:25-37.

Love the Lord your God ... heart, soul, strength + mind

1. Consider the standard that Jesus sets in 10:27-28. Do you think it is possible to live up to it? If 'yes', how? If 'no', then why does Jesus set this standard?

   humanly impossible
   It is the standard God expects & which law lays down
   Failure to meet it drives the sinner / tax collector / us to
   seek Jesus' forgiveness & salvation.

2. What sort of person is the lawyer, and what verses in the passage make you think this?

   expectation of lawyers already poor. + negative!
   v25 - stood up to test Jesus.
   v 29 - wanted to justify himself

   The point of the story criticizes the legal
   attitude of people such as the lawyer.
   ★ who is a 21st lawyer?

3. Imagine that you are the priest or the Levite. List as many reasons as you can why it might be a mistake to help the wounded man (for one reason, see Numbers 19:11).

   touching dead body = unclean for 7 days.
   in a hurry
   didn't want to get involved (help would be ongoing,
   costly
   find himself under attack

4. Do you think any of the reasons you listed in question 3 would also apply to the Samaritan? Are there any other reasons why the Samaritan might have had second thoughts about helping the man?

All the same!
Samaritans & Jews hated each other.

5. Since the Samaritan is Jesus' example of 'how to love your neighbour', what do his actions tell us about <u>what love is like</u>? How could you put this into practice: *✻ see P52 for definition.*

   a. at home?
   loving whatever – against the odds.
   sacrificial

   b. at work or study?

   c. at church?
   Ask about diff. relationships?
   Are there people who we would not pursue a friendship/
   relationship with, because they are too hard?

6. Go back and think about your answers to question 1. Do you still agree with what you said? Why or why not?

7. How does Jesus himself show neighbourly love:

a. in his life? *healings, exorcisms etc. in Gospels relationships, went out of our way.*

b. in his death (compare Luke 5:30-32 and Luke 19:10)?
Without counting the cost, Jesus goes to the cross to die for us —while we are helpless in our sins — Haly dead! Jesus succeeds where we fail!

 ## To finish

Pick one point from Luke 10:25-37 that you think is particularly important. State the point in a way that would make sense to a self-centred teenager, and show where you got it from in the passage.

P 1889   The Message / Remix Bible

Pray

Pray about your own relationships, and those of others in the group.

Radiator

4. LISTENING

Luke 10:38-42

 Getting started

Make a list, in order of importance, of what you consider to be necessary for your life and enjoyment (e.g. food, water, clothing, strong coffee). Explain why you put the top 5 in the order you did.

💡 Light from the Word

Read Luke 10:38-42.

1. Does the story of Martha and Mary seem irritating or unfair to you? Why or why not?

2. What hints do we get about:

    a. the type of person Martha is?

    b. the type of person Mary is?

3. Have a look at the passages below. What are they saying that's similar to the Mary and Martha story?

    a. Luke 8:4-15

    b. Luke 11:27-28

4. How would you reply to someone who said to you:

   a. "Christianity is supposed to be practical, not intellectual. You spend too much time reading your Bible and listening to sermons, instead of helping people."

   b. "Christianity is supposed to be about trusting Jesus, not rushing around trying to do lots of good things. You spend far too much time trying to help people, and going around sharing Jesus with everybody."

   (In answering, don't just give your own opinion. Refer particularly to the passage, and to the other verses in Luke's Gospel that you looked at under question 3.)

5. Think of three practical ideas to help you make time for Bible reading for yourself and/or your family.

 ## To finish

Pick one point from Luke 10:38-42 that you think is particularly important. State the point in a way that would make sense to someone who didn't enjoy reading the Bible, show where you got it from in the passage, and give one illustration.

 ## Pray

Use your answers as the basis for prayer about your Bible reading and sermon listening habits.

5. PRAYER

Luke 11:1-18

 Getting started

What are your prayer habits (by yourself or with others)? Make a list of the main prayer concerns you've had in the last three months, and share them with the group.

*In this session, we will go through the passage twice. On the first run through, we will focus on **who** it is that we're praying to — God the Father. On the second run, we will consider **what** we're praying for.*

💡 Light from the Word

Read Luke 11:1-13.

1. Go through the prayer Jesus prays in verses 2-4. What does Jesus call God?

2. What else can you find out about God and what he's like from this prayer?

3. In the story Jesus tells in verses 5-10, the heavenly Father is compared to an earthly friend.

   a. Imagine yourself as the man in the bed. If you did decide to get up and lend some bread, what would be your reasons?

   b. From the passage, in what ways is God the same as the earthly friend?

   c. In what ways is he different?

4. In verses 11-13, the heavenly Father is compared to an earthly father.

   a. What is Jesus saying about earthly fathers, and what they are like, in these verses?

   b. In what ways are earthly fathers like God? In what ways are they not?

*Re-read Luke 11:1-13, this time focusing on **what** we're encouraged to pray for.*

5. What do you think Jesus means when he says to pray:

   a. "hallowed be your name"?

   b. "your kingdom come"?

   c. "give us each day our daily bread"?

6. Forgiveness is central to God's kingdom.

   a. Have you been forgiven?

   b. Are you good at forgiving people?

   c. How does being forgiven help you to forgive others?

7. Read 11:9. What is this verse encouraging us to ask for (also compare verses 8 and 13)?

8. Go back to your list of common prayer points in 'Getting started'. Compare it with the things Jesus has said to pray for. What do you learn?

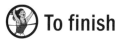 ## To finish

Someone asks you to write a five-minute talk for a breakfast seminar to explain why we pray. What will be your **main point**?

 ## Pray

Pray together as a group, focusing on the things Jesus teaches us to pray for.

6. BEWARE HYPOCRISY

Luke 11:33-12:3

 **Getting started**

"There's no room for rules in genuine Christianity". What do you think? Why?

💡 Light from the Word

Now read Luke 11:33-54.

1. In Luke 11:33-36 Jesus talks about the "eye"—the way we see things. How do people with a "bad eye" see things?

2. What does Jesus say to or about the Pharisees in:

   a. verse 39?

   b. verse 41?

   c. verse 42?

   d. verse 43?

3. How could being a 'religious' person help cover up greed in your life?

4. In Luke 11:47-52, how does the Pharisees' hypocrisy come across in their attitude to the prophets?

5. How does Luke 11:53-54 exactly fulfil what Jesus has just predicted?

6. In Luke 12:1-3, Jesus warns against hypocrisy, and promises that the secrets whispered in private rooms will be exposed. What do you think this has to do with the dinner party that's just been described?

7. Following religious rules and regulations is no guarantee that we are living God's way. In fact, they are a perfect mask for hypocrisy. How can we be sure that we are doing what God wants?

 ## To finish

If someone who had just become a Christian asked you for suggestions on what rules to follow to live a better Christian life, what would you say?

 ## Pray

Consider areas of hypocrisy in your own life. Spend some time praying that you will fear exposure, and understand grace well enough, to avoid hypocrisy.

7. MONEY

Luke 12:13-34

 Getting started

When you have a financial problem to solve, which of these people would you ask for help, and why? (You can tick more than one.)

○ A family member

○ A good friend

○ A financial planner

○ A minister

○ Other

🔆 Light from the Word

Read Luke 12:13-34.

1. What topic is raised by the people who come to Jesus?

2. In Jesus' story, who does the rich man consult for financial advice? What does this tell you about him that is:

   a. positive?

   b. negative?

3. Why do you think Jesus calls the man a fool?

4. If you died suddenly tonight, what do you imagine your friends and family would say about the way you used your money, and your priorities in life? How does the story of the rich fool challenge you?

5. List the reasons in Luke 12:22-34 why we should not be anxious about food, clothing or money:

   a. verse 23

   b. verse 24 and verses 27-8

   c. verses 25-6

   d. verses 29-30

   e. verse 31

   Which of these reasons do you personally find most helpful, and why?

6. What can you say from these verses about:

   a. what God's kingdom is like?

   b. what God is like?

   c. where the best treasure is to be found?

7. How should Luke 12:22-34 affect the way you are making your financial decisions at the moment? Do you need to make any changes?

8. In this passage Jesus gives certain examples of how we know God will care for us. In Luke's Gospel, what is the *most* significant way in which God cares for us (see also Luke 5:31-32; 11:2-4, 13; 19:10)?

 **To finish**

A clever eight-year-old from church asks you why non-church kids always have better toys and clothes. Explain what you would say, using Luke 12 to help.

 Pray

Pray, on the basis of what you've studied, that you would seek God's kingdom first.

FOR THE LEADER

What are Pathway Bible Guides?

Following Jesus is the first in our new series of Pathway Bible Guides. This new series aims to provide simple, straightforward Bible study material for:

- Christians who are new to studying the Bible (perhaps because they've been recently converted or because they have joined a Bible study group for the first time);
- Christians who find other studies[1] too much of a stretch.

Accordingly, we've designed the studies to be short, straightforward and easy to use, with an uncomplicated vocabulary. At the same time, we've tried to do justice to the passages being studied, and to model good Bible-reading principles. We've tried to be simple without being simplistic; no-nonsense without being no-content.

The questions and answers assume a small group context, but it should be easy to adapt them to suit different situations, such as individual study and one-to-one.

Your role as leader

Because many in your group may not be used to reading and discussing a Bible passage in a group context, a greater level of responsibility will fall to you as the leader of the discussions. There are the usual responsibilities of preparation, prayer and managing group dynamics. In addition, there will be an extra dimension of forming and encouraging good Bible reading habits in people who may not have much of an idea of what those habits look like.

Questions have been kept deliberately brief and simple. For this reason, you may have to fill in some of the gaps that may have been addressed in, say, an Interactive Bible Study. Such 'filling in' may take the form of asking follow-up

1. Such as the Interactive Bible Study (IBS) series also available from Matthias Media.

questions, or using your best judgement to work out when you might need to supply background information. That sort of information, and some suggestions about other questions you could ask, may be found in the following *leader's notes*. In addition, a *New Bible Dictionary* is always a useful aid to preparation, and simple commentaries such as those in the *Tyndale* or *Bible Speaks Today* series are often helpful. Consult them after you have done your own preparation.

On the question of background information, these studies are written from the assumption that God's word stands alone. God works through his Holy Spirit and the leaders he has gifted—such as you—to make his meaning clear. Assuming this to be true, the best interpreter and provider of background information for Scripture will not be academic historical research, but Scripture itself. We know for instance that Jews and Samaritans hated each other not simply through historical research, but by reflecting carefully and thoughtfully on passages like 2 Kings 17:29, Ezra 4:10 and Nehemiah 4:2. Extra historical information may be useful for the purpose of illustration, but it is unnecessary for understanding and applying what God says to us.

The format of the studies

The discussion questions on each passage follow a simple pattern. There is a question at the beginning of each discussion that is simply intended to get people talking around the issues raised by the passage, and to give you some idea of how people are thinking. If the group turns out to be confident, motivated and comfortable with each other and the task at hand, you may even decide to skip this question. Alternatively, if the group members are shy or quiet, you may decide to think of related types of questions that you could add in to the study, so as to maintain momentum in a non-threatening way.

After the first question, the remaining questions work through the passage sequentially, alternating between observation, interpretation and application in a way that will become obvious when you do your own preparation. The final question of each discussion, just before the opportunity for prayer, could be used in some groups to encourage (say) one person each week to give a short talk (it could be 1 minute or 5 minutes, depending on the topic and the people). The thinking here is that there's no better way to encourage understanding of a passage than to get people to the point where they can explain it to others. Use your judgement in making best use of this final exercise each week, depending on the people in your group.

In an average group, it should be possible to work through the study in approximately 45 minutes. But it's important that you work out what your group is capable of, given the time available, and make adjustments accordingly. Work out in advance which questions or sub-points can be omitted if time is short. And have a few supplementary questions or discussion starters up your sleeve if your group is dealing with the material quickly and hungering for more. Each group is different. It's your job as leader to use the printed material as 'Bible Guides' not as a set of questions that you must rigidly stick to, regardless of your circumstances.

Preparation: 60/40/20

Ideally, group members should spend half an hour reading over the passage and pencilling in some answers *before* they come to the group. Not every group member will do this, of course, but encourage them with the idea that the more they prepare for the study, the more they will get out of the discussion.

In terms of your own preparation as leader, we recommend you put aside approximately *two hours*, either all at once or in two one-hour blocks, and that you divide up the time as follows:

- 60 minutes reading the passage and answering the questions yourself as best you can (without looking at the leader's notes or Bible commentaries);
- 40 minutes consulting the leader's notes (plus other resources, like commentaries). Add to your own answers, and jot down supplementary questions or other information that you want to have available as you lead the discussion. Make sure you write everything you need on the study pages—the last thing you want to do is to keep turning to the 'answers' in the back during the group discussion;
- 20 minutes praying about the study and for your group members.

This 60/40/20 pattern will help you to focus on the Bible and what it's saying, rather than simply regurgitating to the group what is in the leader's notes. Remember, these notes are just that—notes to offer some help and guidance. They are not the Bible! As a pattern of preparation, the 60/40/20 also helps you to keep praying for yourself and your group, that God would give spiritual growth as his word is sown in your hearts (see Luke 8:4-15; 1 Cor 3:5-7).

If, for some reason, you have less or more time to spend in preparation, simply apply the 60/40/20 proportions accordingly.

1. THE TURNING POINT

Luke 9:18-27

▶ Remember: 60/40/20

 ## Getting started

21st-century readers know the ending of the gospel story. As a result, we are often puzzled by the disciples' confusion about what will happen to Jesus. How could they possibly not understand that he is going to die, when he tells them so clearly that he will?

The only part of Jesus' words and actions that the disciples seem to understand correctly is his claim to be the Christ: the glorious eternal prophet, priest and king, who will rule God's people for all time from God's holy city, Jerusalem. It has taken a while—much teaching and many astonishing miracles—for them to come to this realization, and even now they are fuzzy about what it means. It certainly doesn't occur to the disciples that the king chosen by God might be harmed in any way, let alone be crucified as the worst sort of criminal.

The introductory question is meant to help group members understand how the disciples are thinking. Even though we may be surprised by the disciples' slowness to understand what is going on, their thinking is not too different from the way most people today might think when they imagine the great power associated with kings, presidents, prime ministers, dictators, and other rulers.

The more we understand the way the disciples are thinking, the more powerfully we are struck by the realization that Jesus' kingdom is not an earthly kingdom; it's a heavenly kingdom. The way Jesus achieves kingship in this heavenly kingdom is not by military conquest, or by a devious political process, or by popular revolution. It is by giving his life as a sacrifice for the people who follow him.

If as a leader you can help the group to sympathize with the disciples' way of thinking, the final point will be all the more clear.

Studying the passage

Kicking off with question 1, you might expect that Jesus would predict a great victory. He would arrive at the capital city of Israel, Jerusalem, and be welcomed by all. The popular success he has enjoyed across Galilee would then translate into political power. If things continued to go well, the future would involve the removal of the Roman occupation forces and the successful re-establishment of the throne of David, as promised in 2 Samuel 7. Similarly you might expect Jesus to promise his followers that they would share in his kingly rule. This would surely be one of the first thoughts to occur to an ambitious follower after realizing the power that Jesus possessed. This is confirmed by two things: firstly, that Jesus immediately warns his followers not to think like this (Luke 9:23); secondly, by the fact that they almost immediately do (Luke 9:43-48).

However, Jesus doesn't predict anything of the sort (question 2). Rather, he predicts something quite unbelievable to anyone who really accepts that he is a king. He predicts that he will be refused and rejected; so much so, that the representatives of the people he is to rule over will crucify him.

This isn't just hard for the disciples to accept as a political forecast. It's also a major theological problem for them. According to the Old Testament, the king is the righteous representative of God, who upholds the law of Moses (Deut 17:18-20). This same law says that "a hanged man is cursed by God" (Deut 21:23 —crucifixion is a particularly humiliating form of hanging). So here's the problem: how can God's law-keeping king be cursed as a lawbreaker?

The fact that Jesus will die goes to the very heart of why he has come. In Luke 5:31 and Luke 19:10 his mission is made clear in his own words. He has come to heal spiritually sick people, that is, to find and save those who are spiritually lost in sin.

As the leader, you will want to provide some insight into this point without overwhelming group members with detail. It would be enough to point out that Jesus dies as a substitute, taking the punishment for the sins of all those who put their trust in him as their saviour and Lord. This is absolutely essential to his mission and kingship since, if he doesn't die, we can't be saved. Nor can we become followers of Jesus and members of his kingdom.[2]

---

2. Further information on how we see this in Luke's gospel can be found in session 4 of *Simply Christianity*, also available from Matthias Media.

In question 3, Jesus doesn't want to be misunderstood as a political figure or just a miracle worker, with the subsequent interference to his true mission. But is there any danger that this will happen? Yes, certainly. One example of this is in Luke 5:14-16. Here Jesus attempts to prevent the spread of a report of a particularly powerful healing. Even so, many people hear of what he is doing, with the immediate result that Jesus is forced to withdraw into 'desolate places' whenever he wishes to pray.

This understanding of Jesus' mission has consequences for anyone who wants to follow Jesus, as question 4 begins to examine. Jesus promises suffering in the short term, but life and heavenly glory in the long term. He expresses this positively, and then negatively, by pointing out that life and glory will be lost if the person is unwilling to take up their cross daily, or is ashamed of Jesus and his words (9:25-6).

Note the mention of being ashamed of *Jesus' words*. This comes directly after Jesus has just spoken of his suffering, rejection, death and resurrection. Those particular words, and the idea of suffering before glory, are emphasized both by frequent repetition of the prediction (9:43-45, 13:33, 17:25, 18:31-3, 22:22) and by Luke's recording of how these things are then fulfilled (11:53-4, 16:14, 22:2, 22:52-3, 23:10-11, etc.).

In other words, Christians are not simply being called to follow after a particular moral code that Jesus wants to see upheld. What he really requires of us is trust in him, acceptance of his word, and a willingness to be identified with him in his suffering.

There is an opportunity here to ask whether this is what group members thought was on offer when they became Christians. Some churches would teach that we ought to become Christians because of the benefits available to us in this life. Here Jesus teaches that the Christian life is a life of suffering. Undoubtedly some earthly benefits exist (see Luke 18:29-30, for example). But to see them as the reason for becoming Christian is to miss the point entirely. Rather, we are encouraged to weigh the benefits of the life to come against the suffering of this life.

Question 5 continues to look at the implications of following Jesus. The follower is called on to do three things: we are called on (i) to deny self (ii) to take up our cross daily and (iii) to follow Jesus.

As with other comprehension questions, there is no need to spend a lot of time on this once the correct answer has been discovered in the passage. But it would be good to consider what these things look like in practice, either here or later in the study (later is better, because it links naturally to the final questions in the study, but you can play this by ear).

Taking up the cross daily refers not so much to the big decision to become a Christian, as to the many daily small decisions that will follow on from this. Of course, there is no area of life or decision-making that would be exempt if we call Jesus 'Lord'. But the areas particularly highlighted here are those that relate to personal gain, and whether or not we are willing to acknowledge Jesus publicly.

So what will happen if we do or don't follow Jesus? This question can be answered straightforwardly from the passage. The experience of the Christian life could be summarized as 'suffering now, glory then'. The suffering comes as we make daily decisions that are either painful, or bad for our short-term interests: resisting temptation, resisting the pressure that the world puts on us, ignoring and opposing the satanic pressure to disbelieve Jesus' words and promises. Chief among those pressures will be the pressure to deny the name of Christ either directly or by our silence and inaction (see question 6 for further application).

The glory is by and large hidden from our eyes in this life—although notice how immediately after Jesus issues this challenge, the disciples are given a glimpse of the glory in the transfiguration (Luke 9:28-36). Because the glory is hidden from our eyes we can't speak of what it will be like in any detail. But at its heart will be the recognition given to us by the King of Kings, Jesus Christ, when he stands in the presence of his Father. As great a privilege as it is to know God, far greater is the privilege of being known and welcomed by him.

Question 6 invites group members to share how they came to make the decision to follow Jesus. Although the question assumes that group members will be Christian, this is one opportunity to invite people to talk about whether this is really so. Do group members understand that, although their decision and effort is called for, ultimately what saves them is not that effort, but the suffering and death of the Son of Man? The very language of salvation and rescue in this passage suggests our helplessness. If there is any confusion on this point, it would be worth returning to the earlier part of the study and explaining more carefully the reason why Jesus had to die.

The final question allows plenty of room for a wide-ranging discussion of peoples' struggles to follow Jesus. Encourage personal sharing by giving your own examples, listening carefully, and leaving plenty of time for responses.

There may be room for some helpful specific suggestions. For example, if people find it hard to own up to being Christians in the workplace, ask if they talk about going to church when the conversation turns to 'what I did on the weekend'. Or ask parents if they are praying with their children on a regular basis.

Having said this, one danger to watch out for is legalism. It's easy in a discussion of personal sinfulness to find ourselves doing nothing more than giving advice on the how-tos of avoiding error. As helpful as specific suggestions may be, true change comes as we know and experience the grace of Christ. Therefore the focus of the answer should shift away from ourselves to the action and example of the Lord Jesus.

To finish

The idea of this exercise is to help group members crystallize what they have learnt, and there's no better way to do this than trying to explain it to someone else simply. Give the group a few minutes to think about it, and then, depending on how much time you have available, ask a few people to share their ideas.

This is not meant to be a high-pressure assignment. Keep it light-hearted. Emphasize that the point is to help them think about what they have learned.

If time is limited, you may only have time for one or two people to share. There are questions like this at the end of most of the other studies, so there will be plenty of opportunities for others to take a turn. Also, make sure you build time for prayer into your planning. Base the prayer time on the key points that came from your Bible study together—especially the personal and practical concerns that may have emerged from questions 6 and 7.

2. HARVEST TIME

Luke 10:1-24

▶ Remember: 60/40/20

 Getting started

The first question is a diagnostic question, intended to help you as the leader to get a sense for what group members think about evangelism.

Studying the passage

Jesus gives the 72 the same job that he himself has been doing—he wants people to respond to the kingdom of God. God's kingdom—his promised rule on earth through his chosen King—is about to be set up. So, as question 2 picks up, there is a sense of urgency. The kingdom will come about with the death and resurrection of Jesus, which is just around the corner, even though the disciples can't quite comprehend it. The crisis for national Israel is that their king is coming to them, and they haven't recognized him. As God's chosen people, they are being given every opportunity to repent before the judgement falls. This is in line with the Old Testament idea that God's judgement will begin with his own people (Mal 3:1-2, Ezek 9:6).

The response, however, will be mixed (question 3). Some will accept the message; others will reject it. You could follow up this question by asking who it is that is more likely to be accepting, and who is more likely to be rejecting. Astonishingly, it is those with the *most* information about Jesus who appear to be more likely to reject him. Chorazin, Bethsaida and Capernaum are towns in Galilee that have seen a great deal of Jesus and his powerful work. They will be judged. Tyre and Sidon are not even in Israel—Jesus imagines them repenting if they had seen what Galilean towns have seen.

This negative response by the privileged insiders is entirely in line with the hometown rejection Jesus faced when he began his public ministry (Luke 4:16-29). More profoundly, it fulfils the early prophecies in Luke that predict the tearing down of the proud, mighty, privileged and rich, and the raising up of the humble poor (e.g. Luke 1:46-55; 2:34).

In Luke's Gospel, poverty and wealth are not just about how much money people possess (although this is not irrelevant). More significantly, poverty and wealth are taken as an indication of how people stand spiritually. Those who think they are rich in God's eyes, like the religious Pharisees, are destined for judgement. Those who know they are poor—the sinners and tax collectors of Luke 5:30, for example—are the ones who will cry out for and receive the blessing of salvation. Those who reject the kingdom preached by the disciples will be treated as having rejected Jesus (question 4), which in turn means they will be treated as if they had rejected God (Luke 10:16).

Question 5 is not the easiest question in the world to answer, especially for someone who might be new to Christianity, or not very used to studying the Bible. However, we've included it because it raises the very important issue of how we read the Bible—in this particular instance, how we read the Gospels. It's very important for Christians to learn early on that the Bible is not a collection of magic sayings or instructions that can simply be transferred to our lives without thought.

With the Gospels, for example, or with any other narrative parts of the Bible, we can't move straight from what someone does in the story to what we ought to do. Because Jesus went out to a mountain on his own to pray doesn't mean that this should be the normal mode of our daily prayer. Or, in this case, because Jesus sent out the messengers two-by-two doesn't necessarily mean that we ought to evangelize two-by-two.

The key to answering this question lies in understanding where we fit in the timeline of God's plan. The timeline to bear in mind is this:

1. Old Testament—God promises to bless all nations through Israel.
2. Coming of Christ to Israel. Luke 1-4 is full of indications that the birth of Jesus and his ministry will fulfil the promises God has made to his people —e.g. Luke 1:54-5, 1:68-79, 2:25-6, 2:38, 3:4-6, 4:18-19.
3. The death and resurrection of Christ, which will happen in the lifetime of the disciples (Luke 9:27).
4. The outpouring of God's Holy Spirit on Israel, as promised in the Old Testament (Acts 2:14-21, 38-9).

5. The preaching of the gospel to the Gentiles, together with their receiving of the Holy Spirit (Acts 1:8; 10:34-48).
6. The final judgement (Acts 1:11; cf. 1 Thess 5:2).

Because the disciples are at point 2, and we are at point 5, some of the teaching regarding their mission can't be applied to us. In particular, the sense of urgency in the mission of the disciples comes about because Jesus is about to bring in the kingdom of God through his death and resurrection. So instructions about travelling in pairs (most likely because of the immediate hostility that this mission will inflame), carrying no knapsack, moneybag, or sandals, and being in too much of a hurry to observe normal courtesies, all apply to the 72 because the message of Christ's coming must be heard throughout Israel as soon as possible. His death and resurrection are imminent, and after that—as Luke will show in Acts—the gospel will go beyond Israel and out to all the nations. No similar urgency applies today, because the events that inspired this hurried mission have already occurred.

Nevertheless, because it is impossible for Christians to be definite about the timing of judgement day (1 Thess 5:2), we ought to apply the same level of focus and seriousness to everything that Christians now do, especially in regard to evangelism. Judgement was deadly serious for Israel; it remains deadly serious today for all nations and all people. Trusting in God's timing, we don't need to be hurried. But we will hold continually in our minds the sense that the time for people to respond to God's grace is not indefinite. The time is not known, but it is short (2 Pet 3:1-10).

Therefore, warning people of coming judgement, and encouraging them with the hope of forgiveness, should be uppermost in the thinking of all Christians—just as it was for the 72. The message, that "the kingdom of God has come near to you", will be the same today as it was then. It will carry the added force that these words have now been fulfilled in Jesus' death and resurrection. We now have every reason to respond by acknowledging that the Lord Jesus is king over God's kingdom and over our lives. And we should want to tell others.

As well as this we may expect that, just as the disciples met with a hostile response, so will we. Human nature is unchanged. No-one likes to hear that they are under God's condemnation and must repent. So we should not be surprised or put off by hostility to the gospel.

The great encouragement this passage gives us (especially in verse 16) is that those who speak Jesus' message on his behalf are clearly identified as being on the side of God. This reinforces the message of the previous study (Luke 9:26 in particular).

We should hope that people would respond to this same message when we tell them (question 6). Not every response will be positive, but we should expect that some will be. And we should not imagine that a negative response is the same as failure. We should be thankful all the time that we have the privilege of being Christ's ambassadors, and that we will be blessed in heaven by being counted as Christ's servants (see Luke 6:22-23, 9:26).

Whether or not people become Christians is completely and absolutely dependent upon whether or not God chooses to reveal himself to them (question 7). It does not rely on wisdom, intelligence, educational background, or knowing the right people. Indeed, it is more likely that those with none of these advantages ("little children") will receive the privilege of knowing God.

This is a great relief to any evangelist who thinks that a person's salvation relies on them. Still, the normal way God works is to use human messengers, like the 72. If we were to read on in Luke's other book, the book of Acts, we would see that this pattern continues in the mission of the disciples to Jerusalem, Judea, Samaria, and the ends of the earth (Acts 1:8). If God has revealed the truth about himself to us, then we have been given the great privilege of revealing it to others.

To finish

Again, the idea of the final exercise is to help group members crystallize and then verbalize how they have been encouraged by what they've read. Choose a couple of people to share their ideas with the group.

As you talk about, and then pray for, friends who don't know Jesus, remind the group of God's role in people becoming Christians. Since he is the one who ultimately reveals himself to people, we should ask him to do so for our friends and family.

3. LOVE YOUR NEIGHBOUR

Luke 10:25-37

▶ Remember: 60/40/20

 Getting started

The starter question is a matter of opinion, so there's no one right answer. It can be a free-ranging discussion about who counts as 'in' or 'out'. Feel free to have fun with this question; e.g. "Who thinks it would be acceptable neighbourly behaviour to phone up while [insert your favourite TV programme here] was on TV?"

Studying the passage

The first question is asked at this stage of the study not so much to get the 'right' answer—although if it comes that is fine. The point is rather to raise the key issues that the parable of the Good Samaritan will address.

Thus in leading discussion, it is not necessary to quickly resolve any disagreement about whether it is possible to live up to Jesus' standard of neighbourly love. It would be better instead to let the group wrestle with the passage in front of them, and to feel the tension that the question might provoke. You can then return to the discussion at question 7 below, having hopefully achieved a greater insight not only into the point of the passage but also our spiritual condition.

Having said that, the point to which the study is driving—and, in my view, the parable—is that it is humanly impossible to meet the standard that Jesus sets out for neighbourly love. Even the supposedly law-upholding lawyer is exposed as a failure by the story Jesus tells. What hope then for less respectable members of the community? Luke often shows us in his Gospel how those who consider themselves righteous, such as the lawyer in this incident, are deluded.

It may prove useful, if there is time after question 7, to compare this story with the rich ruler of Luke 18:18-30. The rich ruler's question, "What must I do to inherit eternal life?", is almost identical to the lawyer's in Luke 10:25. The rich ruler, upright and moral as he is, fails to reach the required standard. Jesus' comment on this, as he answers the question "Who can be saved?", is: "What is impossible with men is possible with God". In both Luke 10 and Luke 18, the impossibility of us achieving God's standard by our own effort is being emphasized.

As to why Jesus sets the standard he does, the simple answer is that it is exactly the standard that God expects, and which his law lays down. In Luke's Gospel, the failure to meet this standard is what drives 'sinners and tax collectors' (and the reader) to seek Jesus' forgiveness and salvation.

Question 2 trades on the fact that lawyers already have a bad reputation, established by verses such as Luke 5:21, 6:7 , 7:30 and 9:22 (the "lawyers" and the "scribes" refer to the same group). So our expectation is already negative, and nothing in the lawyer's behaviour on this occasion changes our opinion. The reference to "the test" in Luke 10:25 reflects the language of testing used of Satan in Luke 4:2 and 4:12, and like Satan the lawyer receives his answer from Scripture. Luke also indicates that his main desire is to "justify" himself (Luke 10:29). Likewise the point of Jesus' story criticizes the legalistic attitude of people such as the lawyer (cf. Luke 6:6-11).

Group members can let their imaginations run riot in question 3. To help the beaten man would be inconvenient, costly and risky. The helper himself might find himself under attack. Moreover, if the victim was dead (and according to verse 30 he appeared to be), then according to Numbers 19:11 the one who touched him would become ceremonially unclean. Inconvenient to say the least!

All the reasons listed under question 3 also apply to the Samaritan (question 4). As well as this, Jews hated Samaritans, and Samaritans hated Jews (compare Luke 9:51-56; see also 2 Kgs 17:24-41, and Neh 4:1-9). What's more, how foolish of the Samaritan to effectively hand the innkeeper in Luke 10:35 a blank cheque!

 Question 5 concerns the nature of love. Perfect love is costly and knows no boundaries of class, culture or religion. It doesn't consider what people deserve but what they need. It is frightening to consider because it knows no limits.

It would be good to ask people to be specific and honest about how difficult it is to be a true neighbour. Ask about relationships that they find difficult or perhaps have never even considered, whether at work or school or some other context. Ask whether there are people that we would not really consider pursuing friendship with because they are just too hard. Consider, too, how people have been neighbours to you.

The amount of time you spend on question 6 will depend on how people responded back at question 1. It will be important to help group members see that while the standard is not any less than we would expect of a perfect and holy God, neither is it something that sinful humans could ever hope to achieve.

A good way to answer question 7 would be to consider the examples of healings and exorcisms and other encounters in the Gospel so far. One great story showing the contrast between Jesus and the Pharisees at this point would be Luke 7:36-50.

Jesus shows exactly the sort of love the Samaritan in the story showed. Without counting the cost he goes to the cross to die for us while we are helpless in our sin—half dead! Jesus succeeds where we fail.

This is a very important question for understanding the parable of the Good Samaritan rightly within the Gospel of Luke. Without it, the temptation is to turn the parable into a nice story with a moral, or else to respond to it with despair, since we can't be as loving as we're supposed to be. The individual incidents within the Gospel of Luke must be understood not just on their own terms, but in the context of the Gospel as a whole.

4. LISTENING

Luke 10:38-42

▶ Remember: 60/40/20

 Getting started

The starter question is a way of getting into what people consider to be important. In the incident featuring Mary and Martha, the world's priorities and ways of relating to Jesus are turned on their head.

Because the passage is only 5 verses long, it provides a great opportunity for close study. Every word matters. This is always true, but there is greater opportunity to demonstrate it in this study.

Studying the passage

Most people's first reaction to hearing this story is that it's not right that one should do all the work while the other sits and listens. That is worth getting people to say, but push the group—both in question 1 and in the next question— to look at the detail of the passage.

The passage suggests that Martha is welcoming (v. 38; question 2). This in itself is a very good thing. The word for "welcomed" is the same word as is used of Zacchaeus' delighted welcoming ("receiving") of Jesus in Luke 19:6. Also, compare Jesus' comments on Simon's less-than-generous hospitality in Luke 7:44-47, and also the way in which (in Luke 10) those who welcome Jesus and his disciples are commended and seen as welcoming the kingdom.

The immediate context is especially significant. Jesus has just finished pub-licly roasting a lawyer who loves to play with words but has to be shown, through the story of the Good Samaritan, that words by themselves are not sufficient: words must be accompanied by action (especially words about loving your neighbour!). But the story about Mary and Martha qualifies this by helping us to see that we are not simply to be activists.[3]

However, Martha is *anxious*, as her actions, her words, and the response of Jesus suggest. Martha is distracted not just with "serving", but as the passage says, with "much serving". It was excessive hospitality, beyond what was required by the situation. When she speaks, even though it is only one verse, she mentions herself three times. And her concern is not to listen to Jesus; she gives him an instruction. Her behaviour is an illustration of being overwhelmed by the "cares" of Luke 8:14 (indeed the Greek word translated as "anxious" in Luke 10:41 is nearly identical).

Having said this, her actions still reveal a high regard for Jesus. True, Jesus has delivered a rebuke, but it is not a stinging and condemning rebuke of the type that the Pharisees so regularly receive from him. It is a gentle but firm response and correction to her complaint, and its underlying attitude.

In this story Mary is presented as the model follower of Jesus, carefully attending to his words. She exemplifies the sort of choice that Jesus calls on people to make in Luke 9:57-62.

Notice the exact words used to describe what Mary is doing. She is not just sitting; she is listening. What's more, she is not just listening to Jesus talking about the weather; she is listening to his "teaching"—literally, in the Greek, his "word". This repeats and illustrates the points made in Luke 8:15, 8:21, 9:26 and elsewhere about the significance and importance of hearing, trusting and obeying the 'words' of Jesus.

Thus Mary is not simply slacking off while her sister gets on with the real work. She is doing what Jesus wants his true followers to do.

As a general comment, it's almost certain that Martha and Mary are the sisters referred to in John 11-12, where they are portrayed as trusting in Jesus as the one who has the power to heal and give life. The personalities of Mary and Martha in John are certainly consistent with the personalities of Mary and Martha in Luke 10. You may like to point group members to this cross-reference, so that they can read it in their own time.

As possible follow-ups to this question, you might add: Mary is listening to Jesus speak (v. 39). How do we know she has got it right? What would you say is 'good' about what Mary has chosen (v. 42)?

---

3. Incidentally, this reinforces the line of interpretation taken in the previous study; the story of the Good Samaritan is not simply a morality tale about the standards Christians are meant to live by. We must first receive God's grace and forgiveness.

In question 3, some passages are suggested for comparison. Luke 8:4-15 contains the parable of the soils. Mary and Martha illustrate this parable by showing us two different ways of hearing the word of God. Knowing that Martha is someone who welcomes Jesus is a good reminder to all Christians that we are not to assume that we always attend well to God's word, even if we have put our trust in Jesus. Because of the principles spelt out in this parable, the Mary and Martha story is not just an interesting historical event. It is an example of how to respond rightly (and wrongly) to Jesus' word.

Luke 11:27-28 makes a similar point in a different context. Notice that the blessing comes for those who "keep" the word. The Greek might also be translated 'guard'. It is far more than the idea of simply doing what one is told; rather it is holding onto and trusting and responding to what Jesus says. There is no conflict between being a hearer and a doer in Luke's Gospel. Right hearing leads to right 'doing'; wrong hearing leads to wrong action. Even more significantly, wrong actions —as for example by the Pharisees—can lead to not hearing or recognizing Jesus as the Lord who brings salvation and rescue.

If you wanted to, you could stage question 4 as a debate between the two views. However you choose to handle it, push group members to work hard at the passage and not to leap off to their own ideas or to other parts of the Bible. You want people to see from the examples of Mary and Martha (and to some extent by referring to the immediate context of the story of the Good Samaritan) that priorities, attitudes and actions will all be shaped by the hearing of God's word. They are not to be separated off from each other. Nor will there always be the one right way to respond to what we hear. Sometimes we will need to act, as did the Good Samaritan. Sometimes it will be better to sit and listen, like Mary. Historically speaking, some Christians may have used this passage to promote the monastic or contemplative lifestyle. That, however, is to misunderstand the point, which is responding rightly to Jesus and what he says.

As a summary question, you might ask: "What is the relationship between trusting (that is, listening to) Jesus, and doing the right thing?"

5. PRAYER

Luke 11:1-13

▶ Remember: 60/40/20

 Getting started

The aim of listing prayer habits here is not to encourage legalism, or a guilt trip; and we should be wary of the danger of pride as well (that is, boasting of how much we pray, as opposed to Jesus' exhortation to pray 'in secret'). The point is just to get the group thinking and talking about prayer in their lives. What are their prayer habits? What concerns tend to dominate their prayers?

In this study we go through the same passage twice. Why? Because studying the Bible is not like reading a newspaper—something we skim through, pausing perhaps to read something in detail, and then forget about. It's a bit more like reading the instruction manual for an expensive and highly-tuned piece of equipment we've just bought, whether a sewing machine, a new car or a computer (pick the illustration depending on your group!). You can skim-read for the sheer pleasure of enjoying what you now own. Or you can go through step by step to make sure you really know how to get the most from your new gadget. The genuinely enthusiastic person will probably do both, and do it often until they master the topic. Christians will never 'master' God, so reading and re-reading his word will be a continual delight to us. This study gives a taste for how a passage can profitably be re-read from two angles.

Studying the passage

God is addressed as Father (question 1). The name suggests a deep closeness of relationship with us as his children—a closeness that is encouraged by the attitude of Jesus to his own Father on this and other occasions. The special privilege of being allowed to address God in this way is highlighted when we recall the statements Jesus made back in Luke 10:21-23. No-one except those who know God through Jesus Christ have true knowledge of him. But those who do have true knowledge of him also have the wonderful privilege of being called his children.

Jesus' prayer also teaches that God is a sovereign, generous provider of everything we need. If he is not sovereign, or if he is not generous, there is no point at all in asking him for things. He would be either too weak or too stingy to answer.

The point about the man disturbed in his bed (question 3) is that he would normally act out of friendship, and because the rules of hospitality required it. In the story Jesus tells, the "impudence" (or "persistence") of the one asking for bread plays a role too.

The man asking for bread does seem pushy, to us at least. But consider also the situation: it is a rural village, transport is on foot or at best by donkey, and a traveller has no alternative but to depend absolutely on the hospitality of the villagers. What's more, you couldn't be a genuine Israelite and not travel, because God's law required regular trips to Jerusalem for temple worship. So, not to show hospitality would be a far more serious decision to make then, than it would be today in an urban setting.

Add to this the ordinary demands of friendship, which are being emphasized here (notice that the word 'friend' is mentioned four times in four verses), and it is hardly surprising that the man in bed would get up and provide some bread.

The man at the door is like the disciples, who have just been encouraged by Jesus to pray to God for 'daily bread'. And the man in bed, however, is like God. And God is in the same relationship to us as the man in bed is to his friend at the door: he has the power to grant the request, and the power to refuse. The big difference is in the willingness of God to help. The earthly friend eventually gets up and hands over the bread, despite some initial unwillingness because of the inconvenience. If even the reluctant and complaining earthly friend won't let us down, we can be even more certain that God won't fail us. This is a powerful encouragement.

Jesus' comment on earthly fathers is that they are evil (v. 13; question 4). Even so, they certainly know how to care for their children. In a similar way to the story of the friend in bed, the power of this story comes because it is unthinkable that a father would act in any other way than for the good of his children.

So earthly fathers are the same, in that they do their best to care for their children. But they are different, in that God is able to do a far better job of it than we are. He knows us better, he loves us better, and he has all the resources of creation at his disposal.

Some people doing this study may have had bad experiences with their fathers. Whether the experience has been good or bad, it's important to point out that Jesus teaches us here what true fatherhood is like. God is shown here not as distant, cold and authoritarian. He is generous, loving and kind in the way he exercises his rule. In other words, he shows us the character of a real father, and how a real father ought to behave towards his children. We mustn't work the other way round, and imagine that God is like the flawed examples of fatherhood we might have seen.

"Hallowed be your name" (question 5) means that the one praying wants God's name—his character and his reputation—to be known and held in honour by all. We should know who he is, recognize him as king over all, serve him accordingly, and beg his forgiveness for having failed to honour him and serve him in the past.

The dishonouring of God's name was a constant prophetic charge against the leaders of God's people—see Ezekiel 36:20-21 for example.

What's more, the Gospel of Luke has already given us many examples of how God's name is not being honoured, even (or especially) by the people who should honour him the most. It has been very clearly seen in Luke 10, which speaks in verses 21-24 about how the Father has been revealed to "little children" (Luke 10:21). By contrast, Chorazin, Bethsaida and Capernaum have been condemned. Then the lawyer of Luke 10:25 is exposed as someone who knows God's word but is unable to see its implications for actions and for relationship.

So the prayer is not only a timeless wish that God would be honoured. It's a very specific request that God would be honoured as he fulfils his mission through Jesus and so keeps the Old Testament promises that he's made. In the Old Testament, the promise that God's people, who trust in God by welcoming his Messiah and hearing his word, will be saved; those who fail to trust and instead oppose God's messengers (in Luke's Gospel, Jesus together with his disciples and their message) will be judged.

In practice, the request "your kingdom come" (question 5b) is not too different from the request that the Father's name would be "hallowed". However, its focus is a little different. This request shifts away from the reputation and character and knowledge of God, to the task that Jesus has come to perform.

For a good sense of what God's kingdom looks like, read Luke 1:32-3, 4:43; 11:20, 13:29; 18:25; 23:38, 42. You could ask group members to look at these verses, or summarize them yourself. Ultimately, God's kingdom is a heavenly kingdom brought about by the proclamation of the good news by Jesus, and his coming into glory through his death on the cross. The defeat of demons, the healings and the other signs of power are indications of Jesus' kingship, and the peace, security, prosperity and forgiveness that this kingdom will involve.

The request that God would "give us each day our daily bread" is based on the fact that God is a loving father who can be called upon to give us what we need to live. Literally, the ESV footnote is correct in saying that the prayer is for "our bread for tomorrow". The points of application remain the same: we are asking God to give us enough that we would have no concern at all for the future, because we know that he will supply our immediate needs. Given the stress on the coming kingdom, there may also be the idea that we are trusting God to provide a heavenly banquet for us—as pictured, for example, in the parable of Luke 14:12-24.

Those who trust in Jesus have shown the way forward in chapter 10, where the 72 go out to work for the kingdom with nothing more than what they are wearing. Martha, by contrast, in 10:38-42 has shown an over-preoccupation with the details of daily bread. In the chapters to come we are about to see that the greedy Pharisees, and others, are far too concerned about money, food and clothing.

Question 6 is really intended to discover where people's confidence regarding forgiveness lies.

Forgiveness depends on God, not us. He's the one we offend against when we sin (cf. Luke 5:20-22). As with the other requests in this prayer, God is the only one who can ultimately answer—a point reinforced by the story of the friend in need and the comparison with earthly fathers. So whether or not we have been forgiven can be answered by considering whether or not we have asked to be forgiven. If we have, God is trustworthy and has answered our need. Luke's Gospel leaves us in no doubt that the reason Jesus came was to bring forgiveness of sins to those who look for it (Luke 1:77, 4:18, 5:31-32, etc.).

It's important to clarify a potential confusion. The prayer Jesus teaches isn't suggesting that people's forgiveness *depends* on whether or not we forgive others. When we consider who it is in Luke's Gospel who won't forgive, we quickly realize that it is the Pharisees and lawyers—like the man in Luke 10:29 who desires to "justify himself". These sorts of people want to condemn those who aren't living to the legalistic standard set down by the religious leaders. They have no forgiveness in their own hearts, and they end up being too proud to seek the forgiveness that Jesus freely offers to all. It's not that such unforgiving people can't be forgiven. It's that they refuse to ask for forgiveness and so they won't be forgiven, although Luke's Gospel gives us several examples where the door to forgiveness remains open (e.g. Luke 7:36-50).

Question 6b, about forgiving people, is an opportunity for personal sharing. But even more, it is an opportunity to remind each other that we are to follow God's example in showing grace to each other. God is gracious; those who truly understand and receive his grace will show grace to others.

In its particular context, Luke 11:9 is encouraging us to seek for the fulfilment of our need (question 7). It is not a blanket statement, to encourage us to pray for a larger house and a Mercedes Benz. The story which leads into it (vv. 5-8) is about bread, the meeting of the most basic requirements.

Having said this, both the immediate context and other parts of Luke (Luke 4:4 —"Man shall not live by bread alone") remind us that far greater concerns than just food for bodily survival are on view. Jesus has already told his disciples to pray for the coming of the kingdom. And in the concluding verse of this section (11:13), he tells the disciples that they should rather expect that when they ask God, he will provide his promised Holy Spirit.

Exactly what this means will have to wait until Luke's second volume, Acts, before it becomes really clear. But in Acts 1-2, the promise of the Spirit is dramatically fulfilled and made available to not only the twelve disciples but to everyone who trusts in Christ (Acts 2:38). There it is clearly linked to the forgiveness of sins, and the intention is that this forgiveness should be preached to all the nations of the world—first Judea, then Samaria, then the ends of the earth (Acts 1:8).

However, even if we only look at the passage in front of us (and as a rule that is a good discipline to maintain in every study), it is apparent from its position at the end of the section that the promise of the gift of the Spirit summarizes and concludes what Jesus has just been teaching. The Holy Spirit comes to those who trust in God—that is where the rule of God's kingdom begins.

If people have been paying attention to the passage, it will have helped them to see that our prayers should be shaped by God's concerns, not ours. Question 8 highlights this. At the same time, they ought to have a liberating sense of being able to pray for anything and everything. If God is Father, we don't need to fear him or censor what we say to him.

6. BEWARE HYPOCRISY

Luke 11:33-12:3

▶ Remember: 60/40/20

 Getting started

In this passage Jesus exposes the corrupt heart that lies behind much rule-based religion. Genuine trust and love of Jesus reduces and cuts away at rule-making. The Old Testament laws are a set of rules. But as Jesus deals with the Old Testament laws, we see him consistently interpreting them to show what they truly mean, and what they are pointing to. The Pharisees, as this passage will show, liked to add rules to the existing rules. But the rules they added frequently undercut the whole intention of the Old Testament laws, by dealing with trivia and ignoring the important matters like justice and the love of God.

Studying the passage

Firstly, how do people with a "bad eye" see things (question 1)? The term translated as "bad eye" could equally well be translated as "evil eye" or "greedy eye", both of which help us to see that Jesus is talking here about the basic moral character of the person with the good or bad eye. Some commentaries refer to details of how first century people understood the anatomy and function of the eye. This is unnecessary, and potentially confusing, so don't be tempted to go down this sidetrack. The point here is that your perspective on life will affect how you see things. In particular, here and elsewhere in Luke's writing, it is about a person's spiritual state as it affects their response to God (see Luke 1:78-79, Acts 26:18). Those who are blinded by their greed will not be interested in obeying the law of God or in recognizing his Son.

Even though some in the group might find these few verses a bit unusual, it is worth uncovering the (simple) point being made, because it leads into the condemnation Jesus is about to unleash. Notice the link made in verse 37: "while Jesus was speaking". Verses 37-54 show up the religious Pharisees as people who are deeply affected by the "evil eye".

In verses 39, 41, 42 and 43, Jesus uncovers how the underlying corrupt motivation—the evil eye—is at work among the Pharisees. They are motivated by greed (v. 39) when they should be generous (v. 41). They are worried about appearances and have completely forgotten about what God really wants.

This (question 2) is an observation question and doesn't have to be discussed in great detail. As a leader you might throw in extra detail about the Pharisees from Luke 5:21, 30; 6:2, 7; 7:30, 36-50. These passages reinforce their concern for appearance, their pride in their standing before God and others, and ultimately their refusal to hear, accept and trust God's word and so receive forgiveness.

The main point of question 3 is that religious rules are of little benefit in helping us be like Jesus, even though many people will be impressed by religiosity.

The evidence for this in the passage is that the Pharisees are condemned by Jesus as being highly effective at impressing others, and yet ineffective at living God's way. Paul's comment about religious rules in Colossians 2:20-23 is a good summing up. "These [rules] have indeed an appearance of wisdom ... but they are of no value in stopping the indulgence of the flesh." The underlying problem is refusal to hear God's word (see next question), and it is not helped by introducing religious rules. Indeed, as we see here, religious rules can be a great way of avoiding what God really wants of us.

Thus the specific answer to this question is that being a religious person can mask greed by deflecting people's attention from what is really going on in someone's life. The most likely victims of this deception are religious people themselves, who will tend to be proud of their own performance and judge others against it. Greed can also be masked by religious rules, in that those rules appear to be dealing with the problem they are covering, like an expensive medicine that has no effect.

The Pharisees' attitude to the prophets (question 4) is similar to that of gangsters who send bouquets to the funerals of their victims. The Pharisees seem to honour the prophets by building expensive tombs for them. But they are fundamentally opposed to their message, from Abel to Zechariah—the whole range of prophets from first to last. (The 'A to Z' of Abel and Zechariah is a nice coincidence only!) Not surprisingly, then, the Pharisees hate what Jesus has to say. He speaks "the Wisdom of God" and exposes them.

The real problem is that the Pharisees won't hear God's word (compare Luke 7:30, and Luke 20:9-19). They are proud of their standing as insiders, but they refuse to acknowledge their own Lord, and what he has to say to them through the prophets, and now through Jesus.

Contrast this with what we've seen previously about how God's followers are marked out by hearing, trusting, accepting and acting on Jesus' words.

There is a hint in Jesus' words and actions that the Pharisees might even repent (question 5). After all, Jesus has turned up to eat with one of them, and not for the first time. Eating dinner with someone leaves the door wide open for friendship and acceptance, even though the Pharisees seem to have used it as a way to get close enough to Jesus to judge him.

What's more, Jesus has specifically told the Pharisees what they need to do to win God's acceptance (vv. 41, 42). Even now, they have the opportunity to repent and receive Jesus and his words in the way they should.

However, the Pharisees fail. The clarity with which Jesus speaks only makes them angrier, and escalates the conflict to another level. They are now out to get him (v. 54), fulfilling Jesus' words about how they oppose the prophets. You could follow this question up by asking, "How does the story end?"—in other words, the Pharisees and religious leaders finally succeed in killing Jesus.

In answering question 6, notice how Jesus is effectively promising that the hypocrisy of the Pharisees will be exposed.

Depending on how cluey your group is, you could follow up this question by asking, "When is the hypocrisy of the Pharisees exposed?" Answer: It is exposed when the Pharisees fail in their plan to keep Jesus dead. When he rises again, Luke records how Peter proclaims: "God has made him both Lord and Christ, this Jesus whom you crucified" (Acts 2:36). That is, when God raises Jesus from the dead, the Pharisees are clearly seen to be in the wrong. The resurrection confirms everything Jesus says about them.

We can be sure of being right with God because of the grace of God revealed in Jesus (question 7). This is the only guarantee that we are living as God pleases, because it depends not on our own performance but on God's kindness and generosity in forgiving our sins and giving us his Holy Spirit.

In Luke's Gospel, the challenge again and again is to rightly accept the words of Jesus and follow after him. This means accepting that we are sick and sinful, and need his healing and forgiveness. And, as we saw in the previous study, those who ask, receive.

7. MONEY

Luke 12:13-34

▶ Remember: 60/40/20

 ## Getting started

As well as starting discussion, the initial question should give the attentive leader many helpful clues as to how their group members make practical financial decisions, and where gospel priorities fit in.

Studying the passage

The specific issue in question 1 concerns a property dispute.

Money and greed are highly significant and related topics in Luke's Gospel. You could easily reach the view that having money and having salvation are mutually exclusive (e.g. Luke 1:53-54; 6:24). However, it's not that straightforward, as the mention of Solomon in this section (12:27) reminds us. Solomon is one of the richest men in the Old Testament, along with other faithful leaders of God's people such as Abraham, Joshua and David. Indeed these people are rich because of their trust in God, not in spite of it.

Also in Luke's Gospel, we discover that Jesus is supported in his ministry by a group of wealthy individuals (Luke 8:1-3), and that he singles out the wealthy Zacchaeus for table fellowship (Luke 19:1-10; Zacchaeus then promptly signals his repentance by giving his money away!).

The real issue is greed, as it is impossible to serve both God and money (Luke 16:13).

The rich man (question 2) consults only himself (vv. 17-19)! As an exercise, get the group to count how many times in these verses the rich man speaks of "I". Ask them if they know any people like this.

The reader (or group leader) who is paying attention is entitled to ask whether or not the rich man has any family or friends, and if so, where they figure in this picture. The rich man is completely self-absorbed and selfish. God figures nowhere in his plans, and there is no mention of the poor and needy people who could have benefitted from the rich man's generosity (see Deut 15:7-8). Notice that as Jesus tells the story, it is not the rich man's hard work that produces a result, rather, it is "the land ... [that] ... produced plentifully".

About the only positive thing that might possibly be said is that the man does plan ahead for how to deal with his huge harvest (cf. Prov 6:6-8). But even this faint praise fails because he intends simply to live the life of a sluggard. More significantly, as Jesus reveals, he is going to die that night. His wisdom has carried him only as far as his present earthly existence, and he fails to consider God and the coming judgement (cf. Luke 12:5).

The rich man is a fool because he is a practical atheist (Ps 14:1; question 3), who doesn't fear the Lord (Prov 1:7). In the immediate context of Luke's Gospel, he is a fool because he is one of those who thinks his life consists "in the abundance of his possessions" (Luke 12:15).

For question 4, you might ask people to write an imaginary two-minute speech (given by a relative) at their own funeral. You could roleplay this with a volunteer, if there is time, or simply ask people to mention the key points.

Question 5 is both an observation question and an opportunity to probe deeply on the application of the passage. The ultimate reasons for not worrying relate to the character of God—a sovereign and gracious Father—and the reality that worry about money changes nothing.

Rather than being concerned about food and clothing, Jesus says that we should be concerned for God's kingdom (Luke 12:31). This passage locates God's kingdom beyond earthly, physical concerns (question 6a). It's not that those concerns are trivial—God's kingship means that these concerns for food and clothing will be met, and far more, without us having to chase after them or be anxious about them. Even in those situations where persecution means we're deprived of what we physically need, we can take consolation in the reality that our treasure is in heaven, that is, with God. (In study 5, you may have already looked at some of the following references earlier in Luke to God's kingdom: Luke 1:32-3, 4:43; 11:20, 13:29; 18:25; 23:38, 42).

It's a kingdom which has first call on our allegiance, which should come first in our priorities. Luke 12:15 and Luke 12:23 remind us of some words quoted earlier in Luke's Gospel: "Man shall not live by bread alone" (Luke 4:4; quoting Deut 8). Yet this doesn't stop us looking to God for our daily bread (Luke 11:3, and compare the blessings also on offer in Luke 4:18-19). What does sustain us, as Jesus' quote from Deuteronomy reminds us, is attending to God's word. The full verse of Deuteronomy 8:3 reads: "And he humbled you and let you hunger and fed you with manna, which you did not know, nor did your fathers know, that he might make you know that man does not live by bread alone, but man lives by every word that comes from the mouth of the LORD".

This passage confirms that God is sovereign, that he is gracious, that he cares deeply for our needs (and not only for ours, but for the needs of the whole of creation—Ps 104:27), and that he can be depended upon to act accordingly (question 6b). Nevertheless, as our sovereign Lord he is also our judge, and will judge us according to where our allegiance lies, whether to earthly treasure or heavenly treasure. True treasure is found in heaven, that is to say, with God. He is the source of true wealth and gives us the life we need to enjoy it (vv. 32-34).

Question 7 is an application question and deserves to be followed up with others:

- What do people do when they are under financial pressure?
- How do they react to worry about money?
- What are some examples of people at church who have reacted well?
  (The group will be encouraged by your example, if you are able to share failures as well as successes.)
- How can the group help each other to deal with pressure better?
  (E.g. They might find out what the pressures are, remind each other of God's grace and his promises, and make concerns a matter for prayer, and in some cases specific action to help.)
- How do our spending habits reveal our priorities?

Finally, question 8 is there to remind us that, according to the gospel, the most significant way that God cares for us is to act through Jesus to save us from sin.

Don't be tempted to think of this question as an optional extra in a Bible study that is really just about money. Luke's constant speaking against the evils associated with money and possessions are not there simply to persuade us about giving up capitalism, or aiming for a simple lifestyle. They may or may not be decisions we decide to make for ourselves.

However Luke's concern—which is Jesus' concern—is that unrighteous, lost, sinful human beings may have their eyes opened to their terrible state before God, and seek heavenly treasure by begging him for forgiveness. God will care for us in good ways by giving us food, clothing, and drink. He cares for us in the best way of all by giving us the word of life through the cross of Christ, and inviting and demanding that we turn from serving ourselves to serving him.

matthiasmedia

Matthias Media is a ministry team of like-minded, evangelical Christians working together to achieve a particular goal, as summarized in our mission statement:

> *To serve our Lord Jesus Christ, and the growth of his gospel in the world, by producing and delivering high quality, Bible-based resources.*

It was in 1988 that we first started pursuing this mission together, and in God's kindness we now have more than 250 different ministry resources being distributed all over the world. These resources range from Bible studies and books, through to training courses and audio sermons.

To find out more about our large range of very useful products, and to access samples and free downloads, visit our website:

www.matthiasmedia.com.au

How to purchase our resources

1 Through a range of outlets in various parts of the world. Visit **www.matthiasmedia.com.au/contact/overseas.htm** for details about recommended retailers in your part of the world.

2 Direct from us over the internet:
 – in the US: www.matthiasmedia.com
 – in Australia and the rest of the world: www.matthiasmedia.com.au

3 Direct from us by phone:
 – within Australia: 1800 814 360 (Sydney: 9663 1478)
 – international: +61 2 9663 1478

4 Trade enquiries worldwide:
 – email us: sales@matthiasmedia.com.au

More Pathway Bible Guides

Pathway Bible Guides aim to provide simple, straightforward Bible study material for:

- Christians who are new to studying the Bible;
- Christians with lower literacy levels who find other studies too much of a stretch.

We've designed the studies to be short and easy to use, with an uncomplicated vocabulary. At the same time, we've tried to do justice to the passages being studied, and to model good Bible-reading principles. Pathway Bible Guides are Bible studies that are simple without being simplistic; no-nonsense without being no-content.

Standing Firm
1 Thessalonians

Peace with God
Romans

Getting to Know God
Exodus 1-20

Genuine Imitation

Genuine Imitation is, without doubt, one of the most exciting and innovative resources for many years. This interactive study on CD-ROM is designed to help you unpack Paul's first letter to the Thessalonians in a way that is both highly informative, yet so simple.

With just a click of your mouse, open a world of audiovisual presentations and commentaries. Explore the meaning, background and key themes of each passage and see how it applies to us all today. You can even jot down notes to create your own study based on this timeless letter of encouragement to stand firm in Christ from Paul.

FOR MORE INFORMATION OR TO ORDER CONTACT:

Matthias Media
Telephone: +61 2 9663 1478 | Facsimile: +61 2 9663 3265
Email: sales@matthiasmedia.com.au

www.matthiasmedia.com.au

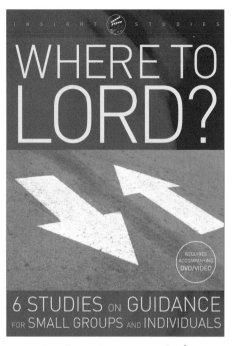

Beyond Greed

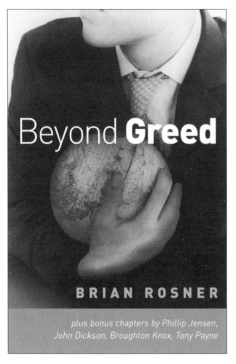

'Greed' is not the most fashionable concept these days. It ranks with 'guilt' and 'sin' as words that many modern people have virtually stopped using.

According to Brian Rosner, greed is also a massive blind spot for Christians, which is surprising given how much the Bible has to say about it. He writes:

The most disturbing thing about the fact that greed is idolatry is that hardly anybody owns up to being a worshipper. Imagine the response of disbelief in the local church if it were revealed that the vast majority of its members were secretly worshipping other gods. Yet if our analysis of the religion of money is right, the unthinkable may not be so far from the truth.

Beyond Greed helps open our eyes to the problems, and proposes a liberating lifestyle that trades in greed and materialism for something of far greater worth and satisfaction.